Baltimore
A History in Postcards

Mary L. Martin
and Nathaniel Wolfgang-Price

Schiffer Publishing Ltd®
4880 Lower Valley Road, Atglen, PA 19310 USA

The Beneficiaries

Pediatric Oncology Friends is grateful to Mary Martin Postcards for naming it a beneficiary of royalty proceeds from this book.

Johns Hopkins Pediatric Oncology Friends was founded in 1990 to raise funds for pediatric cancer research. The volunteer organization has raised over $1 million to fund the Hopkins research team.

"When you lose a child to cancer, it's so very difficult because you're losing a future and all of the dreams you had for that child," says Friends founder, Ginny Mitchell. "We're learning more and more everyday. The money we raise now will impact the lives of children today and one hundred years from now. What we accomplish tomorrow is built on what we learn today. Pediatric Oncology Friends is determined to make the future brighter for all children."

Those wishing to learn more about or make a donation to Pediatric Oncology Friends can do so through the Sidney Kimmel Comprehensive Cancer Center at Johns Hopkins University or at http://www.hopkinskimmelcancercenter.org.

Library of Congress Control Number: 2006924845

Designed by Mark David Bowyer
Type set in Impress Bt / Korinna BT

ISBN: 0-7643-2489-6
Printed in China

Published by Schiffer Publishing Ltd.
4880 Lower Valley Road
Atglen, PA 19310
Phone: (610) 593-1777; Fax: (610) 593-2002
E-mail: Info@schifferbooks.com

For the largest selection of fine reference books on this and related subjects, please visit our web site at **www.schifferbooks.com**
We are always looking for people to write books on new and related subjects. If you have an idea for a book please contact us at the above address.

This book may be purchased from the publisher.
Include $3.95 for shipping.
Please try your bookstore first.
You may write for a free catalog.

In Europe, Schiffer books are distributed by
Bushwood Books
6 Marksbury Ave.
Kew Gardens
Surrey TW9 4JF England
Phone: 44 (0) 20 8392-8585; Fax: 44 (0) 20 8392-9876
E-mail: info@bushwoodbooks.co.uk
Website: www.bushwoodbooks.co.uk
Free postage in the U.K., Europe; air mail at cost.

Contents

About Baltimore

Introduction

During the seventeenth century, a number of towns named Baltimore were founded around the upper portion of the Chesapeake Bay. The towns were named after Cecil Calvert, the Second Baron Baltimore and the first Proprietary Governor of Maryland. The town known today as Baltimore, Maryland was chartered and laid out in 1729—almost one hundred years after the first European settlers arrived in Maryland. Baltimore-Town grew and prospered, becoming a key port along the East Coast and a leader in shipbuilding.

One of the most important moments in Baltimore's history came in 1814 during the War of 1812's Battle of Baltimore when a young lawyer and amateur poet, Francis Scott Key, observed an American flag flying over Fort McHenry. The flag and the fort had both survived an intense bombardment by invading British ships, and the sight of the battered banner still proudly waving over the fort inspired Key to write a poem entitled, *The Defence of Fort McHenry*—a poem that would later be set to music, renamed "The Star Spangled Banner," and become the National Anthem of the United States of America.

Despite the hardship imposed on the city by the Civil War, Baltimore moved into the twentieth century with its figurative head held high and more than ready for the challenges of the new century. Even a disastrous fire in 1904 could not dampen the city's spirits, and like the mythical phoenix, Baltimore arose from the ashes and remade itself into a modern and progressive city. This was a city that fascinated and impressed visitors who came to Baltimore riding on the famous Baltimore & Ohio Railroad or taking a leisurely trip down the coast on a steamer. From the suave and elegant 1900s to the fast-paced 1950s and beyond—whether it was for business, pleasure, or just a stop on a longer journey—visitors came to Baltimore to be fascinated by the city's sights, sounds, smells, taste, and unique culture and flavor.

Where tourists came, postcards went. Vintage postcards ranging from the 1900s to the 1950s, sent home by those same visitors, showcase some of the people, places, and things that made Baltimore unique and gave it the nickname, "The Charm City."

Greetings from Baltimore Maryland, "The Greatest City in America."

Circa 1940s, $2-4

A view of Baltimore circa 1800.

Cancelled 1910, $6-7

A bird's eye view of Baltimore, as seen from the top of the Shot Tower.

Circa 1915, $7-9

On February 7, 1904, a fire broke out at the corner of Liberty and Redwood Streets. It burned for roughly thirty hours destroying 1,526 buildings.

Circa 1915 , $10-12

A view of the Baltimore skyline from on top of the Washington Monument at Mount Vernon Place.

Circa 1940s, $4-6

Gutted in the Great Fire, the Hopkins Place Savings Bank was rebuilt and reopened a year later in May of 1905.

Circa 1915, $10-12

Another scene of the destruction left in the wake of the Great Fire. Most of the damaged areas in the city were rebuilt within two years following the fire.

Circa 1910s, $10-12

The new Elks Lodge on West Fayette Street.

Circa 1920s, $6-8

Built in 1828, the Shot Tower is the only tower of its kind left in the world. Shot was made there by pouring molten lead through a screen at the top of the tower. The droplets formed into balls on their way down before landing in a vat of cold water at the bottom of the tower.

Circa 1940s, $2-3

A bird's eye view of the "Sunken Gardens," a small inner city park located near the Standard Oil and New Amsterdam Buildings.

Cancelled 1927, $6-8

Another view of Baltimore's "majestic" skyline.

Circa 1940s, $2-3

The Baltimore YMCA Building, "one of the finest and most complete structures of its kind in this Country."

Cancelled 1927, $4-6

Steamers dock along the waterfront in Baltimore's Inner Harbor.

Circa 1940s, $4-5

The Baltimore skyline at night.

Circa 1940s, $2-3

Ford's, located on Callow Avenue.

Cancelled 1916, $5-7

A stretch of Baltimore's famous red brick rowhouses. The white marble steps were an excellent sales point for real estate agents and a point of pride for many working-class homeowners.

Circa 1940s, $3-5

History

Before Europeans came to North America, the Baltimore area was home to the Susquehannock, an Iroquoian-speaking nation who lived along the Susquehanna River. The first European to visit was Captain John Smith who explored the area that would become the Inner Harbor on his voyage north in 1609, searching for food for the struggling Virginia Colony.

On June 20, 1632, King Charles I of England granted the charter for the Province of Maryland to Cecil Calvert, Second Baron Baltimore. The king had granted the charter to Cecil's father, George Calvert, but it had never been executed due to the latter's death earlier that year. In setting up a colony, Lord Baltimore hoped to set up a haven for persecuted English Catholics and to turn a profit as well. In 1634, the first of the settlers began to arrive in Maryland. The group was largely made up of Catholics, but also included a number of Protestants as well. In an effort to help defuse tension between the two groups, the Maryland Colonial Assembly passed the Maryland Toleration Act that permitted freedom of religious practice (as long as the religion was Christian) within the province's borders.

During Maryland's history, a number of towns named Baltimore were constructed, named after the title of Cecil Calvert, Baron Baltimore who was the colony's founder and first Proprietary Governor. The town that would become the present day Baltimore was chartered and laid out in 1729. Boatloads of immigrants from Great Britain and elsewhere swelled the town's population, and merchants from Northern Ireland brought in additional wealth and leadership.

In 1797, Baltimore-Town merged with the nearby towns of Fell's Point and Jones Town, allowing the towns' leaders to obtain a city charter. The new city of Baltimore continued to grow, encouraged by the money brought in by the deep-water port and shipyards of Fell's Point and through the actions of John Eager Howard who donated large portions of his lands to the city for public use. By 1800, Baltimore had lost most of its village traits and became a growing city.

During the 1800s, Baltimore's fame as a shipyard increased, and a number of ships were built, including the famous Baltimore Clippers that were so popular with American privateers. During the War of 1812, in an effort to eliminate the pirate threat and to further demoralize the American people, the British attacked Baltimore by land on September 12 and by sea on September 13, 1814. A witness to the attack by sea, Francis Scott Key, inspired by the sight of an American flag waving triumphantly over Fort McHenry, sat down and wrote the poem that would eventually become the National Anthem of the United States of America.

Emboldened with its defiance of the British, Baltimore continued to grow. New streets were laid out, new buildings were built, and Baltimore Clippers traveled the ocean trade routes carrying goods from Baltimore and the surrounding countryside. In 1828, the Baltimore & Ohio Railroad was founded, making Baltimore as easily accessible by land as by sea.

While the first shots of the Civil War were fired in Charleston, the first blood shed in the Civil War was shed in Baltimore. Officially a slave state, Maryland remained part of the Union. Despite that, most of the state's population—the people of Baltimore included—was largely sympathetic towards the Confederacy. On April 19, 1861, a mob of pro-Confederate Baltimoreans attacked a regiment of Union soldiers traveling through the city. The soldiers panicked and retaliated by firing into the crowd, causing a fierce riot between the soldiers, the mob, and the Baltimore police who were trying to break up the riot. From that point on, until the end of the Civil War, Union soldiers occupied Baltimore, and the rest of the state was placed under Federal administration.

After the Civil War, immigrants from Europe and other parts of the United States came to Baltimore, increasing the city's population and adding to the workforce. The city continued to prosper until February 7, 1904 when the Great Baltimore Fire struck. The fire began at the corner of Liberty and Redwood Streets, burned for over thirty hours, destroyed 1,526 buildings, encompassed seventy city blocks, and left 35,000 people unemployed. However, in spite of the obvious tragedy, the people of Baltimore rose to the occasion by rebuilding the city—making it more modern and more fireproof.

Baltimore moved along with the rest of the nation providing troops, materials, and supplies for World War I and World War II. After World War II, the population of Baltimore rose again as more people migrated to the city from rural areas. Recent redevelopment of the Downtown area has led to a revitalization of the Inner Harbor and other historic districts, which, in turn, has brought more visitors who give the city a much-needed "shot in the arm." In spite of fire, floods, riots, and attacks by British soldiers, Baltimore has remained standing tall and more than ready to face the challenges of the coming years.

Fort McHenry

Fort McHenry was built as part of a plan authorized by Congress in 1794, calling for the building of forts to protect important ports along the east coast of the fledgling United States of America. The fort was built on Whetstone Point (which would later be known as Locust Point), a peninsula jutting out into the Patapsco River. It was designed by Jean Foncin in 1799 and was completed in 1805. The bastion was named Fort McHenry in honor of James McHenry, an Irish Marylander who had been Secretary of War under George Washington.

An important part of Baltimore's defenses, Fort McHenry's moment of fame came during the War of 1812. After sacking Washington D.C., the British forces, under Admiral Sir George Cockburn and General Robert Ross, turned toward Baltimore to capture the port that built and sheltered the ships responsible for harassing British merchant vessels.

On September 12, 1814, General Ross landed his troops on North Point and marched them towards Baltimore. A day later, on September 13, nineteen British ships began bombarding Fort McHenry. The bombardment lasted close to twenty-five hours. On the morning of September 14, an oversized, hastily made American flag still flew over the fort signifying that the defenders had not given up, and the fort was still in American hands. The British then retreated, having failed by land and by sea to capture Baltimore.

On board a truce ship, not too far from Fort McHenry, Francis Scott Key, a young American lawyer, witnessed the bombardment. The next morning, when Key saw the American flag flying intact over the fort and heard the faint sound of the fort's band playing, "Yankee Doodle Dandy," he felt so moved that he composed a poem to commemorate the event entitled, *The Defence of Fort McHenry*. The poem was later put to the tune of an English drinking song called, "To Anacreon in Heaven" and would go on to become the National Anthem of the United States of America.

During the Civil War, Fort McHenry was used as a military prison housing Confederate soldiers and civilians with suspected Confederate sympathies. During World War I, the fort, and the land around it, was used as a hospital to treat soldiers returning from Europe. In World War II, it was used as a Coast Guard base fulfilling its original purpose as part of Baltimore Harbor's defense system.

By 1925, Fort McHenry had been made into a national park. In 1939 it was re-designated a National Monument and Historic Shrine (the only place to have such a double designation), and in 1966 the fort was placed on the National Register of Historic Places. Today, Fort McHenry is one of Baltimore's top tourist destinations, with thousands of visitors coming to view the "Birthplace of the Star Spangled Banner."

Fort McHenry was built as part of a plan to fortify and defend the harbors and ports along the eastern coast of the United States of America.

Circa 1915, $5-7

The entrance to Fort McHenry. The fort was designated a "National Monument and Historic Shrine" in 1939 and was placed on the National Register of Historic Places in 1966.

Circa 1915, $10-12

On September 12, 1814 (during the War of 1812), the British attacked Baltimore by land and by sea. It was the sight of an American flag flying over Fort McHenry, after an intense British bombardment, that inspired Francis Scott Key to write the poem that would later become the National Anthem of the United States.

Circa 1940s, $2-3

An aerial view of Fort McHenry. The fort was designed by the French engineer, Jean Foncin, in 1799, and completed in 1805.

Circa 1940s, $3-4

Fort McHenry was named for James McHenry who was a resident of Maryland and Secretary of War under Presidents George Washington and John Adams.

Circa 1920s, $3-5

Designed and built by Robert E. Lee, Fort Carroll is located on the Patapsco River, south of Baltimore. The fort was abandoned as a military post in 1920.

Circa 1920s, $3-5

The Flag House, where Mary Pickersgill made the flag that would inspire Francis Scott Key to write his poem, *Defence of Fort McHenry*, that would later be renamed, "The Star Spangled Banner."

Circa 1920s, $6-8

Inside Baltimore

Monuments

Baltimore is home to a number of other monuments and statues erected to commemorate events, famous Baltimoreans, Marylanders, and others whose lives and deeds made a lasting impression upon the city.

In particular, the Washington Monument resides in Baltimore—which is not to be confused with the Washington Monument in Washington D.C.—and is the first urban monument dedicated to George Washington. The city is also home to the Battle Monument, which commemorates the soldiers who died in defense of Baltimore during the Battle of North Point in the War of 1812. It is unusual that this monument lists the names of all who died—not just the commander—which went against the custom of the day. Other Baltimore monuments commemorate such notables as John Eager Howard, Francis Scott Key, and Edgar Allan Poe.

Located at Mount Vernon Place, this statue is dedicated to John Eager Howard, a Maryland native who was honored by Congress for his bravery and decisive role in the Battle of Cowpens. He is also known for donating a large amount of land to the city for public use.

Circa 1915, $5-7

Designed and built by Robert Mills, the Washington Monument is over 170 feet tall and was the first urban monument dedicated to George Washington.

Circa 1915, $5-7

Also located in Mount Vernon Place, this bronze lion was sculpted by Antoine-Louis Barye, a French artist well known for his animal sculptures.

Circa 1915, $6-8

Built in 1925, the War Memorial was dedicated to the Marylanders who died during World War I. The building was rededicated in 1977 to also honor Marylanders who died in World War II, the Korean War, and Vietnam War.

Circa 1940s, $3-4

The monument dedicated to Thomas Wildey, who founded the Independent Order of Odd Fellows in Baltimore in 1819.

Circa 1915, $5-7

The monument dedicated to the soldiers and sailors from Maryland who served in the Confederate Army and Navy. The inscription reads, " *Gloria Victis*. To the Soldiers and Sailors of Maryland in the Service of the Confederate States of America."

Circa 1915, $5-7

The monument honoring Francis Scott Key shows the composer in a rowboat presenting his manuscript of "The Star Spangled Banner" to the statue of Columbia on top of the monument.

Circa 1940s, $2-3

Also called the "Maryland Line Monument," the Revolutionary War Monument is dedicated to members of the Maryland Line Regiment who died fighting a delaying action against British troops in Long Island.

Circa 1915, $5-7

This marker stands over the grave of Edgar Allan Poe in Westminster Hall and Burying Ground. His body was moved and reburied closer to the front gate of the cemetery in 1875.

Circa 1915, $4-6

Statue dedicated to the Confederate Women of Maryland. Though officially a Union State during the Civil War, Maryland was home to a number of Confederate sympathizers.

Circa 1915, $4-6

The Battle Monument in Court Square honors the thirty-six soldiers killed in the Battle of North Point in defense of Baltimore during the War of 1812, and was erected in 1815. This was contrary to the custom of the time period in which only the regiment's commanding officer was so honored and noted.

Circa 1940s, $3-4

Located at the end of Mount Royal Avenue, this bronze statue is dedicated to Lt. Colonel William F. Watson who was killed in Monterey, Mexico during the Mexican-American War.

Circa 1915, $4-6

Statue of Cecil Carroll Calvert, Second Baron Baltimore, who was the first Proprietary Governor of the Province of Maryland.

Circa 1915, $3-5

Another view of the Baltimore War Memorial and Plaza, which is also dedicated to Marylanders who died in World War I, World War II, the Korean War, and the Vietnam War.

Circa 1940s, $1-3

Mount Vernon Place and the Washington Monument.

Circa 1915, $5-7

Statue dedicated to Roger B. Taney, the fifth Chief Justice of the United States and the brother-in-law of Francis Scott Key.

Circa 1915, $4-6

Monument in Harlem Park dedicated to James L. Ridgely, the founder of the first Odd Fellows lodge.

Circa 1915, $5-7

A monument in Wyman Park dedicated to Edgar Allan Poe, who lived in Baltimore for a short time and died there in 1849.

Circa 1915, $4-6

The Union Soldiers and Sailors Monument in Druid Hill Park. During the Civil War, Maryland was officially a Union State, but individuals from Maryland fought on both sides of the conflict.

Circa 1915, $5-7

Baltimore Harbor

The heart of any port city is its harbor, and for Baltimore, this is especially true. From the 1700s to the 1970s, the harbor was the home of a major United States seaport. From the 1970s on, the harbor, particularly the Inner Harbor, was reinvented as the cultural center of the city, and a good number of Baltimore's tourist attractions are located there.

The first people to make use of the Baltimore Harbor were Susquehannock Indians, who fished and hunted for waterfowl in the bay. When English colonists began arriving in Maryland in 1634, Baltimore Harbor became the favorite shipping point for tobacco grown in southern Maryland. It was not until after the Revolutionary War that Baltimore Harbor became known as a major port.

Besides being a major port, the harbor was also home to a sizable shipbuilding industry centered around Fell's Point, and was the birthplace of the "Baltimore Clipper," a type of ship known for its incredible speed.

Baltimore Harbor was also home to a sizable steamer fleet. Companies like the Old Bay Line, the Chesapeake Line, the Ericsson Line, and the Merchants and Miners Transportation Line would offer trips to cities, including Annapolis, Norfolk, Richmond, Philadelphia, and Boston, as well as return trips to Baltimore. This proved to be a popular mode of travel, and by the early 1900s, the Baltimore Harbor was crowded with steamers from dozens of companies making runs all over the East Coast—and even a few across the Atlantic.

The fire boat, *Deluge*. Boats like these are an important part of the fire departments in port cities like Baltimore.

Circa 1915, $8-10

The Light Street Wharf, as seen from the Harbor.

Circa 1915, $7-9

A view of the Light Street Wharves from the landside. After the Great Baltimore Fire in 1904, the wharves were rebuilt and the street was widened.

Circa 1915, $10-12

Workers build the Standard Oil Company's Pier. This kind of growth around the harbor was common after the Great Baltimore Fire.

Circa 1915, $8-10

The second United States naval ship to bear the name, the USS *Constellation* was commissioned in 1855 and built in Norfolk, Virginia. It is currently moored in Baltimore Harbor and serves the city as a museum ship and tourist attraction.

Circa 1915, $7-9

The Lazzareto Lighthouse was once part of an April Fool's Day prank played by Edgar Allan Poe who posted a fake announcement in the paper claiming that a man would fly from the top of the Shot Tower to the lighthouse.

Cancelled 1908, $10-12

The grain elevators and piers in Canton Harbor.

Circa 1915, $8-10

The Baltimore and Ohio Company Docks at Locust Point.

Circa 1915, $8-10

Another view of the Baltimore & Ohio Railroad Pier.

Circa 1900, $12-15

Baltimore was home to a sizable fishing industry. Here, fishermen unload freshly caught Chesapeake Bay oysters into fish market wagons.

Circa 1915, $10-12

The steamer *Louise* makes its way across the Chesapeake Bay. A number of Baltimore steamship lines made overnight runs to Annapolis and Norfolk.

Circa 1915, $7-9

The United States Revenue Service Pier.

Circa 1915, $10-12

The Fruit Pier on Pratt Street, where the produce shipped to Baltimore was unloaded and sent to grocers and markets throughout the city.

Circa 1915, $10-12

Unloading melons at the Fruit and Vegetable Wharf.

Circa 1915, $10-12

The Oyster Wharf, also located on Pratt Street.

Circa 1900s, $10-12

The Ore Docks owned and operated by the Maryland Steel Company and located on Sparrow's Point.

Circa 1915, $9-10

A view of Baltimore Harbor as seen from the top of Federal Hill.

Circa 1915, $8-10

Excursion steamers crowd the docks on the waterfront.

Circa 1910s, $7-9

One of the city's largest excursion steamers, the *Express* made the run from Baltimore to Tolchester from 1925 to 1933.

Circa 1910s, $7-9

Replacing the *Express*, the *Tolchester* made the run from Baltimore to Tolchester from 1948 to 1955.

Circa 1940s, $5-7

The *Annapolis*, one of the many excursion steamers that sailed to and from Baltimore.

Circa 1915, $8-10

Often called, "Baltimore's favorite steamer," the steamer *Louise*, enters a berth at the Light Street Wharf.

Circa 1915, $10-12

Another harbor scene.

Circa 1915, $10-12

Baltimore's oyster fleet. Oysters were particularly plentiful in the Chesapeake Bay and very popular throughout the Bay area and beyond.

Circa 1915, $8-10

Because of its natural harbor, Baltimore was a destination for many private ships as well as commercial shipping and fishing traffic.

Circa 1915, $12-15

Besides fishing boats and excursion steamers, Baltimore also saw a fair amount of ocean liner traffic.

Circa 1915, $10-12

A typical scene along the Baltimore wharves.

Circa 1915, $7-9

Skinners Dry Dock. Baltimore was home to a sizable shipbuilding industry at Fell's Point.

Circa 1915, $10-12

Public Buildings

Like many other historical cities, Baltimore has its share of impressive public buildings. One of the oldest is City Hall, which was built in 1875 and then renovated a hundred years later in 1975. Other famous public buildings include the Enoch Pratt Free Library and the Clarence M. Mitchell Jr. Courthouse. Most of the public buildings are located in the City Hall District, which has been the seat of the city's government since Baltimore's colonial days.

In 1985, the courthouse was rededicated in honor of Clarence M. Mitchell Jr., one of Baltimore's most prominent Civil Rights activists.

Cancelled 1919, $5-6

Built in 1900, the Clarence M. Mitchell Jr. Courthouse was constructed on the site of the first two courthouses erected in the city.

Circa 1915, $8-12

City Hall was designed by George A. Frederick and built in 1875.

Circa 1940s, $2-4

The Baltimore Post Office.

Circa 1915, $5-6

Water Tower on Roland Avenue, near the city line.

Circa 1915, $6-8

Located in the City Hall District, the Municipal Office Building housed a number of city and government offices.

Circa 1920s, $5-7

Besides being an armory and a convention hall, the Fifth Regiment Armory is also home to the Maryland National Guard Museum.

Circa 1940s, $2-4

The Fifth Regiment Armory. Formed as a small militia in 1774, the Fifth Regiment has fought in every American war, except the Civil War.

Circa 1920s, $5-6

The Baltimore City Jail was designed to give the prisoners housed inside as much sunlight and air as possible and was criticized as being "a palace for felons."

Circa 1915, $10-12

In the late 1800s, Enoch Pratt, a prominent dry goods merchant, gave the city the Enoch Pratt Free Library, one of the first of its kind in the country.

Circa 1920s, $5-6

The interior of the Armory. It was in this hall that Woodrow Wilson was nominated by the Democratic Party to be their candidate for the 1912 Presidential Election.

Circa 1915, $6-8

Hospitals

Baltimore has a long and fascinating medical history. Perhaps the most famous medical institution in Baltimore is the internationally renowned Johns Hopkins Hospital. When Baltimore businessman, Johns Hopkins, died in 1873, he left $3.4 million (a very substantial sum for the time) towards the establishment of a medical school and hospital to care for the citizens of Baltimore and the people living in the area around the city. The hospital that grew out of Hopkins's grant became one of the best in the country, introducing new procedures and techniques in the practice, as well as the study and the teaching of medicine that revolutionized the medical field of the day.

Named after its benefactor, Johns Hopkins Hospital has become one of the most prestigious hospitals in the world.

Circa 1915, $6-8

The second largest shareholder in the Carnegie Steel Company, Henry Phipps was a philanthropist who donated money to a number of charities and helped fund a number of public buildings like the Henry Phipps Psychiatric Clinic of the Johns Hopkins Hospital pictured here.

Circa 1915, $6-8

The Franklin Square Hospital.

Circa 1915, $6-8

The Baltimore Marine Hospital. This hospital, and others like it, was established in port cities to provide health care for merchant marine sailors and to fulfill a number of other public health functions.

Circa 1940s, $2-4

The Baltimore City Hospital and College of Physicians and Surgeons.

Circa 1915, $6-8

The Church Home and Infirmary on North Broadway.

Circa 1915, $6-8

A teaching hospital, the University Hospital is part of the University of Maryland.

Circa 1940s, $2-4

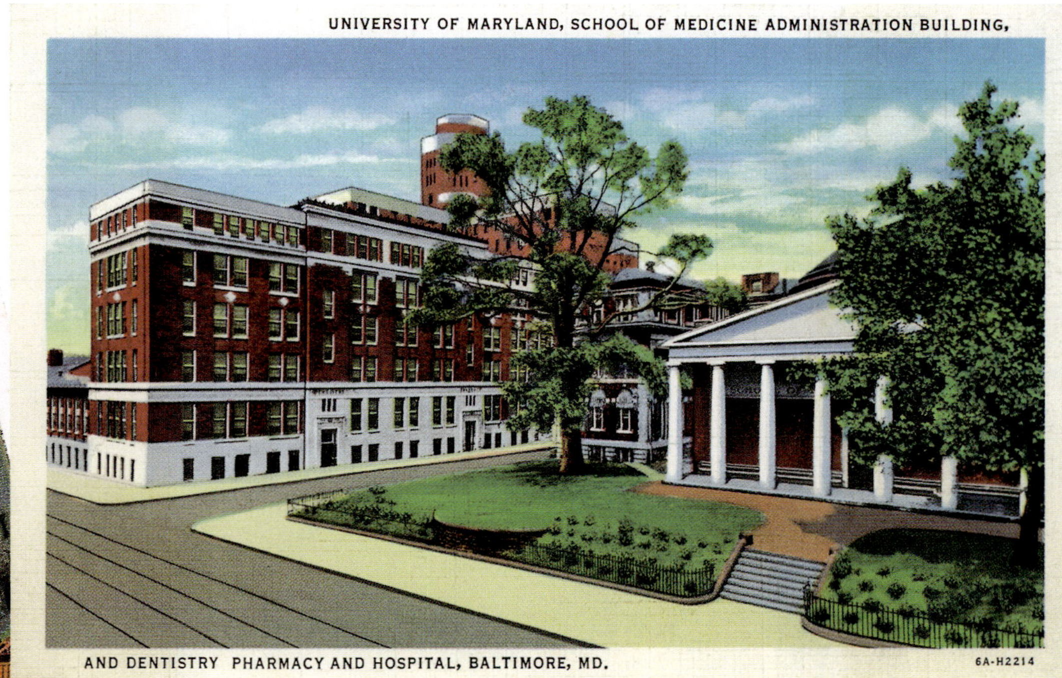

The Administration Building of the University of Maryland's School of Medicine. Also pictured are the Dentistry and Pharmacy buildings as well as the Hospital.

Circa 1940s, $2-4

The Union Memorial Hospital, Johnston Hospital and Nurses Home.

Circa 1940s, $3-4

In the past, men and women were treated in separate hospitals, and many hospitals were established solely for the treatment of women—like the Hospital for Women of Maryland in Baltimore.

Circa 1915, $6-7

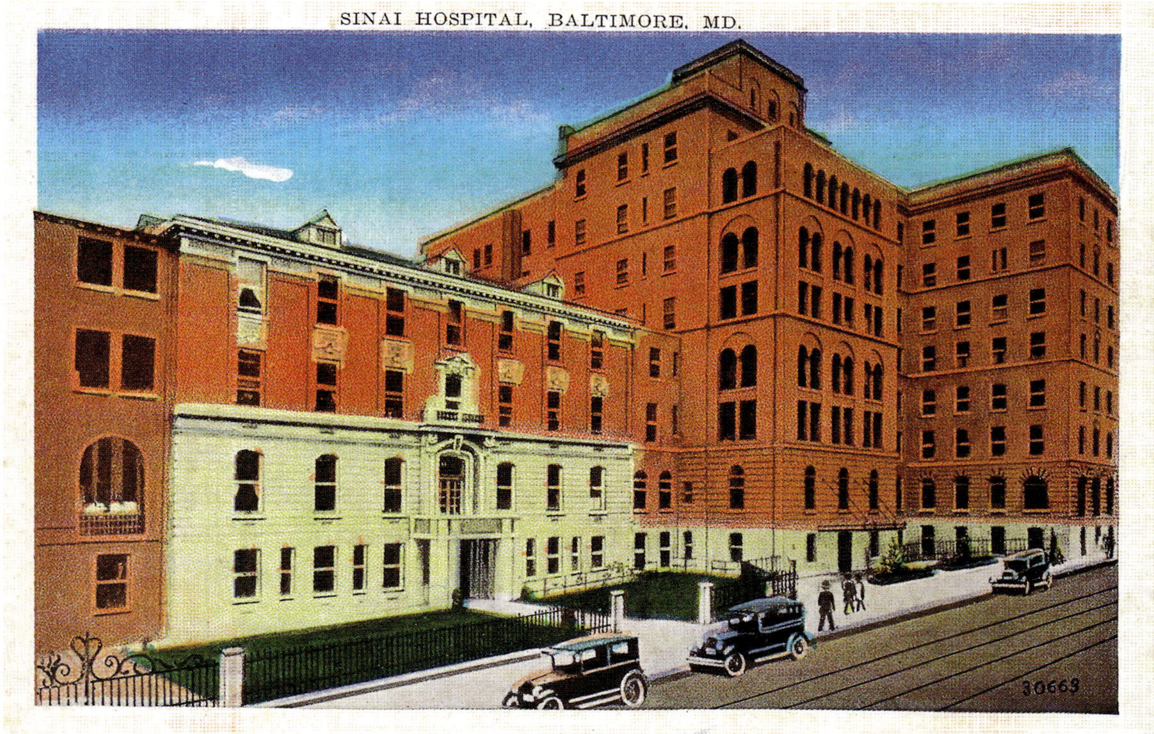

The Sinai Hospital.

Circa 1920s, $5-6

The Hebrew Orphan Asylum was established in 1872 and built on land donated by William S. Rayner, a local Jewish Businessman.

Circa 1915, $7-8

Churches

When Cecil Calvert set about to establish the Province of Maryland, one of the goals he had in mind was to set up a haven for British Roman Catholics who were facing increasing political and social persecution back in England. However, it was determined that more settlers would be needed to make the colony thrive, which meant that Protestants would have to be included. To further ease the tension between Catholic and Protestant settlers and authority figures, Maryland's Colonial Assembly passed the Maryland Toleration Act in 1649. This made the tolerance of other Christian denominations mandatory throughout the colony, making Maryland one of the most religiously diverse English colonies at the time. In 1789, the Catholic Church appointed Baltimore as the diocese for the entire United States—the first diocese in the United States. Baltimore is home to the Basilica of the National Shrine of the Assumption of the Blessed Virgin Mary, the first Catholic Cathedral built in the United States.

The First English Lutheran Church.

Circa 1915, $6-7

The Episcopalian Pro-Cathedral.

Circa 1915, $6-7

Located on Charles and Thirty-fourth Streets, University Baptist Church was designed by John Russell Pope.

Circa 1915, $6-7

Saints Phillip and James' Church. The colony of Maryland was founded as a haven for British Catholics, and because of that, cities like Baltimore have a high Catholic population.

Circa 1915, $6-7

In 1649, the Colonial Assembly of Maryland passed the Maryland Toleration Act. This established legal protection for other Christian denominations allowing churches like the Associated Congregational Church to be established.

Circa 1915, $6-7

A view of the Francis Scott Key Monument and the Eutaw Place Temple.

Circa 1940s, $3-4

The current St. Paul's Episcopal Church on Charles and Saratoga Streets is the fourth church built on that spot.

Circa 1915, $6-7

The Lutheran Deaconess Motherhouse, one of the three major centers of the Deaconess Community of the Evangelical Lutheran Church of America.

Circa 1915, $6-7

The Passionist brothers of St. Joseph's Monastery came to Baltimore in 1865. The monastery was dedicated in 1886.

Circa 1915, $6-7

The Scottish Rite Temple of Freemasonry is located on Charles and Thirty-ninth Streets and was designed by Clyde N. Friz and John Russell Pope.

Circa 1915, $6-7

St. John's Episcopal Church in Mt. Washington.

Circa 1915, $6-7

The first Catholic cathedral built in the United States, the Basilica of the National Shrine of the Assumption of the Blessed Virgin Mary was designed by Benjamin Latrobe, the architect who also designed the United States Capitol Building.

Circa 1920s, $5-6

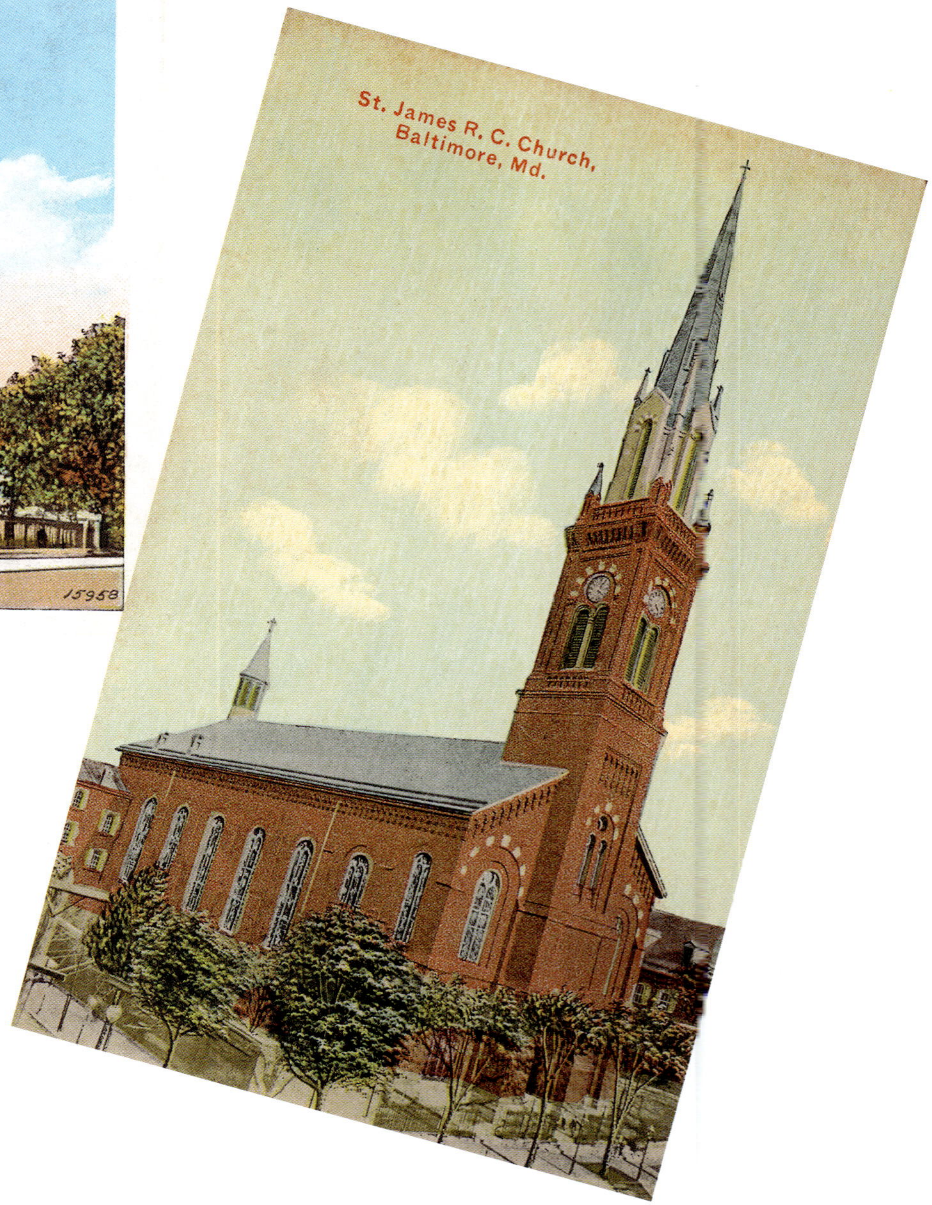

At 256 feet, the spire of St. James and St. John's Church is one of the tallest church spires in the city.

Circa 1915, $6-8

St. Martins Catholic Church, on the corner of Fayette and Fulton Avenues.

Circa 1915, $6-8

St. Ann's Roman Catholic Church and School.

Circa 1915, $5-7

Westminster Presbyterian Church. Edgar Allan Poe is buried near the gate of the churchyard.

Circa 1915, $6-8

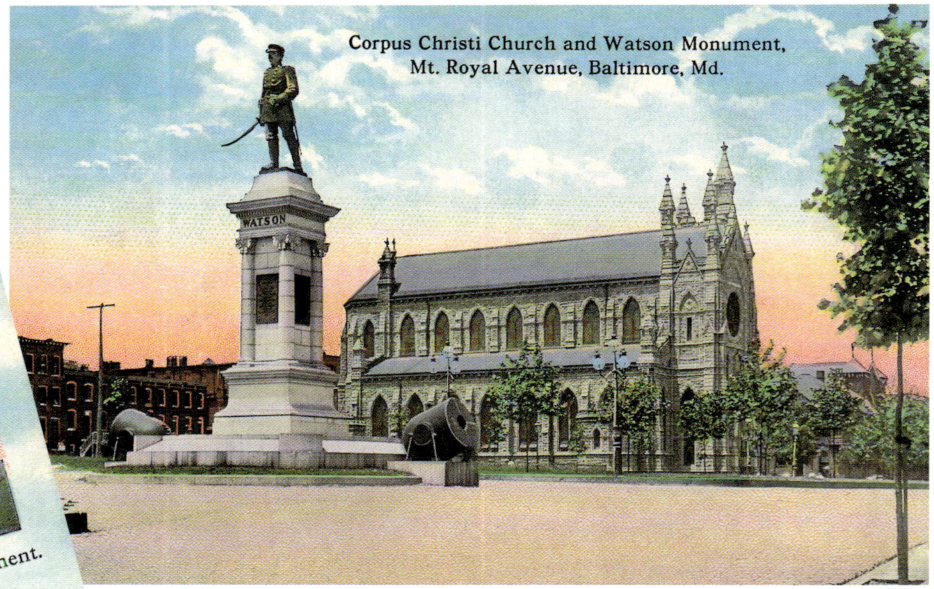

Originally called the Jenkins Memorial Church, the Corpus Christi Church was built by the Jenkins family in memory of banker and railroad magnate, Thomas Courtney Jenkins.

Circa 1915, $6-8

Built to house the Archbishop of Baltimore, the Archbishop's House is connected, by private entrance, to the Basilica of the National Shrine of the Assumption of the Blessed Virgin Mary next door.

Circa 1915, $6-8

Schools

By the end of the Civil War, Baltimore was more than able to serve the educational needs of its citizens. However, it was not until the latter part of the nineteenth century that the city's educational system experienced a rapid upsurge in growth. Schools like the Brynn Mawr School for Girls, Eastern and Western High Schools, and the Polytechnic Institute were all opened during that time period.

Besides elementary and secondary schools, Baltimore also serves as the home for a number of institutes of higher learning: Johns Hopkins University, for example, funded by the famous philanthropist, Johns Hopkins; the University of Maryland School of Medicine, home to Davidge Hall, the oldest building in the country that has been continually used for medical education; the Maryland Institute College of Art, recognized as one of the finest art schools in America; and the Peabody Institute, the first music academy established in the United States.

In 1871, sail maker and businessman, Samuel Ready, died leaving the majority of his property towards the establishment of an orphanage for girls.

Circa 1915, $6-8

The Samuel Ready School opened in 1887 on a sixteen-acre lot on North and Hartford Avenues.

Circa 1915, $6-8

Originally called the Boys Manuel Training School, the Baltimore Polytechnic Institute received its present name in 1893.

Circa 1920s, $5-7

The famous bands of St. Mary's Industrial School.

Circa 1915, $12-15

City College was erected in 1928 and cost $2.5 million to build, a sum many considered too extravagant for a school building.

Circa 1940s, $1-3

The Maryland Institute Building was one of the first air-conditioned buildings ever constructed, with fans blowing over blocks of ice in the basement sending cold air circulating through the building's ducts.

Circa 1920s, $5-7

After the first building was destroyed in the Great Baltimore Fire, philanthropists Michael Jenkins and Andrew Carnegie both donated funds in order to build a new Maryland Institute Building on Mount Royal Avenue.

Circa 1915, $6-8

Another view of the Maryland Institute, founded in 1826. It is the oldest accredited art college in the United States.

Circa 1920s, $5-7

The Baltimore Medical College was founded in 1881 as a teaching hospital. It affiliated with the University of Maryland School of Medicine in 1911.

Circa 1900s, $6-8

Opened in 1839, Baltimore City College is the third oldest public high school in the United States.

Circa 1930s, $5-7

The oldest Roman Catholic seminary in the United States, St. Mary's Seminary was founded by Sulpician Fathers in 1791. The present building was built in 1927.

Circa 1915, $6-8

Forest Park High School.

Circa 1920s, $4-6

Western High School began as an all-girls school.

Circa 1920s, $4-6

Goucher College was founded in 1885 as the Women's College of Baltimore. According to legend, the architects designing the College's main hall laid out the building in the shape of an "E" as a memorial to Eleanor, John and Mary Fisher Goucher's daughter who had died at a young age.

Circa 1910s, $3-5

Maryland State Normal School. The school was renamed Towson State Teacher's College when it began offering bachelor's degrees in 1935.

Circa 1915, $6-8

Gilman Hall, located on the Homewood Campus of Johns Hopkins University, was named after the University's first president Daniel Coit Gilman.

Circa 1920s, $3-5

Built in 1812 and named for Dr. John B. Davidge, the founder and first dean of the University of Maryland School of Medicine, Davidge Hall is the oldest medical school building still in use in the United States.

Circa 1915s, $5-7

A view of the University of Maryland, showing the Dental Department, the School of Medicine, and the Law Department.

Circa 1915, $5-7

Located inside the Peabody Institute, the "Cathedral of Books" is home to approximately 250,000 books and has been called one of the most magnificent public spaces in Baltimore.

Circa 1915, $7-9

The Peabody Institute was founded by George Peabody in 1857 and was the first music academy to be established in the United States.

Circa 1915, $5-7

Streets

In 1729, the town of Baltimore received its charter, and plans were drawn up to determine the layout of the growing town. The streets were laid out in a grid pattern. As the city grew, the number of streets increased and the existing ones were expanded to fit the growing city's needs—still maintaining a grid pattern but branching out in different angles according to the lay of the land.

After the Great Fire of 1904, the streets, along with the rest of the city, were given a more modern upgrade. They were paved and widened to make them more uniform and to create more space for growing carriage and automobile traffic. Streets like Baltimore Street redefined themselves as new businesses and buildings were erected to replace the ones damaged or destroyed in the fire.

Baltimore Street, looking west from Hopkins Place, showing a section of Baltimore's manufacturing and wholesale district.

Cancelled 1920, $9-12

Another view of Baltimore Street, this one looking west from Calvert Street.

Circa 1915, $10-12

Broadway, looking south from North Avenue.

Circa 1915, $5-7

A view of North Broadway, showing the Wildey Monument in the background.

Cancelled 1913, $6-8

Lower Broadway Street, leading to the Broadway Market and Broadway Pier.

Circa 1915, $12-15

A view of Broadway, showing some of Baltimore's famous marble-stepped rowhouses.

Circa 1915, $6-9

A bird's eye view of the Saint Paul Street Bridge. Union Station is visible in the background.

Circa 1920s, $7-8

Charles Street Boulevard. A number of the city's more prominent homes were located in this area.

Circa 1920s, $5-7

Motorcars park on either side of Charles Street.

Circa 1920s, $5-7

The Orleans Street Viaduct gave motorists an easier route from Downtown to East Baltimore.

Circa 1940s, $3-5

The Howard Street Bridge extension.

Circa 1940s, $3-5

Charles Street, looking south from Union Station. The Hotel Belvedere and the Washington Monument are visible in the distance.

Circa 1920s, $8-10

A view of Harlem Square showing the Ridgely Monument.

Circa 1915, $5-7

Once the location of the home of Charles Howard, the son of John Eager Howard, Mount Vernon Place has become Baltimore's most famous square. Not only is the Washington Monument found here, but events like the Flower Mart and the Baltimore Book Festival are also held here annually.

Circa 1915, $6-7

In the late 1790s, Union Square was part of Thorowgood Smith's private estate. It became part of the city proper following the construction boom of the 1830s.

Circa 1915, $6-8

Preston Gardens.

Circa 1940s, $3-5

Howard Street was named after John Eager Howard, a Revolutionary War hero and landowner who donated a significant portion of his land towards Baltimore's development.

Circa 1920s, $9-12

Once one of Baltimore's more affluent streets, Eutaw Place was modeled after the *Avenue des Champs-Elysees* in Paris.

Circa 1920s, $5-7

A busy scene on Howard Street as seen from Lexington Street.

Cancelled 1921, $10-12

A number of Baltimore's retail stores were located on Lexington Street.

Circa 1915, $10-12

Lexington Street, Baltimore's "shopping district" as seen from Eutaw Street.

Cancelled 1911, $10-12

A different view of the Orleans Street Viaduct.

Circa 1920s, $7-8

Fallsway, located in the Inner Harbor area.

Circa 1915, $8-10

Stretching over the Patapsco River, the Hanover Street Bridge connects downtown Baltimore with Curtis Bay.

Circa 1940s, $3-5

After the Great Baltimore Fire, Light Street was widened and new buildings and wharves were constructed on both sides of the street.

Circa 1920s, $7-9

Light Street showing the Bay Line Terminal.

Circa 1915, $8-10

Doing Business in Baltimore

In the 1630s, tobacco farmers used Baltimore's natural harbor as a convenient place to load and ship tobacco grown in the southern part of the state. By the 1700s, when the city incorporated, Baltimore was a thriving port, and by 1900, it ranked third among American cities in its volume of foreign trade. As a major port and as the starting point for the Baltimore & Ohio Railroad, Baltimore was ideally suited for the transportation of materials and finished goods. A number of businesses found this to be helpful to their business. Raw materials were constantly being shipped in, and manufactured goods like toys, textiles, canned goods, liquor, and shoes left by both rail and water. Companies like American Sugar and Glenn L. Martin Company took advantage of Baltimore's accessibility by building plants and factories in and near the city to be close to ocean and rail transportation that could both bring in materials and take out finished products. A number of companies also got their start in Baltimore, including the well-known McCormick & Company, which began as a small door-to-door company working out of a cellar and spare room.

One of Baltimore's main imports was sugar from the South and the Caribbean. It was processed and refined in places like the American Sugar Refinery pictured here.

Circa 1920s, $6-8

Making airplanes for civilian companies and for the military during World War II, the Glenn L. Martin Company Aircraft Plant was the largest unit aircraft plant in the United States.

Circa 1940s, $3-5

The Candler Building on the corner of Pratt Street and Market Place.

Circa 1940s, $2-4

Banks like the Metropolitan Savings Bank served the growing number of Baltimore's merchants and businessmen.

Circa 1915, $5-7

Louis Kaufmann & Sons, established 1866.

Circa 1920s, $8-10

McCormick & Company started out in Baltimore in 1889. The factory pictured here was built in 1921.

Circa 1920s, $6-8

The Munsey Building, one of Baltimore's skyscrapers.

Circa 1920s, $5-7

Baltimore's major newspaper, *The Baltimore Sun*, was founded in 1837 by Arunah Shepardson Abell. The newspaper's office is pictured here.

Circa 1915, $6-8

Located on the northwest corner of Baltimore and Charles Streets, the Baltimore & Ohio Building was the headquarters for the Baltimore & Ohio Railroad.

Circa 1940s, $3-4

After it was opened in 1894, the Fidelity Building was only eight stories high. Another seven stories were added to the building between 1912 and 1915.

Circa 1915, $5-7

Opened in 1929, the Baltimore Trust Building is Baltimore's only Art Deco style skyscraper.

Circa 1930s, $3-5

Sears, Roebuck and Company's new Super Store. The store first opened its doors in 1941.

Circa 1940s, $3-4

The Lexington Street Building on the corner of Liberty and Lexington Streets.

Circa 1920s, $6-7

Fifty-one feet tall, the bottle on top of the Bromo-Seltzer Building is ten thousand times the size of a regular bottle of Bromo-Seltzer.

Circa 1920s, $7-9

The Maryland Casualty Building, located on Baltimore Street near City Hall.

Circa 1920s, $7-8

Modeled after the Erechtheum on the Acropolis in Athens, the Saving Bank of Baltimore was nicknamed, "The Temple of Thrift."

Circa 1915, $7-8

Frizzell's Art Rooms, "Baltimore's most popular art store."

Cancelled 1901, $9-10

Markets

The first open-air market in Baltimore was the famous Lexington Market, which was established on land donated by John Eager Howard. Farmers would come from as far away as Towson and Reisterstown to sell and buy meat, butter, eggs, produce, and other goods. Merchants would come from within Baltimore's city limits offering livestock, feed, and other farming essentials. The first real building assembled at Lexington Market was a large wooden shed built in 1803.

Besides Lexington Market, Baltimore offered other marketplace areas like Center and Belair Markets that operated under the same principles as Lexington Market—local merchants and growers gathered to buy and sell produce and other goods. The Fish Market (where fish and shellfish caught in Chesapeake Bay were bought and sold) and smaller individually owned markets also operated in this fashion at Lexington Market, acting as small grocery stores selling produce, and sometimes oysters and fish as well.

Perhaps the most famous market in Baltimore, the Lexington Market was set up on land donated by John Eager Howard and is named after the Battle of Lexington.

Circa 1915, $12-15

This wooden shed was built in 1803 to house stalls in Lexington Market.

Circa 1910s, $9-11

Baskets of potatoes and heads of cabbage are presented for consideration and purchase at Center Market. Produce like this was grown locally in farms outside the city and then brought in fresh by wagons and boats.

Circa 1915, $10-12

The interior of the Baltimore Fish Market. Most of the seafood sold here came locally from the Chesapeake Bay.

Circa 1915, $15-20

An exterior view of the Fish Market. Fish and shellfish were unloaded at the waterfront and brought to the market in wagons like the ones pictured outside the market.

Circa 1915, $15-20

Belair Market was built on land deeded to the city by Nicholas Rogers, the owner of Druid Hill, for five dollars.

Circa 1900s, $10-12

Because of Baltimore's location on the Chesapeake Bay, a number of grocers and markets (like this one) sold both produce and seafood.

Circa 1915, $20-25

Visiting Baltimore

Getting Around the City

The first steamship to sail from Baltimore, the *Chesapeake*, made its first run from Baltimore to Annapolis and back in 1813. But even before that, horse-drawn carriages, buggies, and wagons would clatter up and down dirt roads and cobblestone streets coming in and out of Baltimore. In 1827, the Baltimore & Ohio Railroad was chartered by the State of Maryland. Three years later the Mount Clare Station was built in West Baltimore.

Getting to and from the city was never a problem. The Baltimore & Ohio and Pennsylvania Railroads made daily trips to various points around the country, and the Washington, Baltimore, and Annapolis Electric Railroad offered more short-range service to Annapolis, Washington D.C., and along the South Shore Line. At the harbor, steamers sailed to and back from places as close as Annapolis and as far away as Le Havre, France.

By the 1920s, Baltimore also had an airport, Logan Field. Later on, a more modern facility, the Baltimore Municipal Airport, was built adjacent to Logan Field. It was from this airport that Pan American Airways began flying their fleet of Martin Clippers. An even more modern airport, the Friendship International Airport, was opened in 1950 and was designed to accommodate the new commercial airplanes. The facility was renamed Baltimore-Washington International Airport in 1973 and is still in service offering flights from Baltimore to various points across the United States and around the world.

The New Washington, Baltimore, & Annapolis Electric Railroad Company Station on Howard and Lombard Streets.

Circa 1900s, $10-12

New Terminal Station and train yard for the Washington, Baltimore, & Annapolis Electric Railroad.

Circa 1920s, $12-15

Boxcars sit idle at the Baltimore & Ohio Railroad Freight Yards at Locust Point.

Circa 1915, $12-15

Baltimore's location on Chesapeake Bay and the Patapsco River made the city ideal for boating and other water sports. A number of private boat and yacht clubs like the Arundel Boat Club were headquartered along the bay and the river.

Circa 1915, $8-9

One attraction at the Druid Hill Park was a guided automobile tour of the city.

Circa 1915, $10-12

Cases displaying Baltimore and aviation memorabilia line the main lobby of the Friendship Airport.

Circa 1940s, $8-10

When it opened in 1896, the Mount Royal Station was the largest station ever built to accommodate one line.

Circa 1920s, $6-7

The Washington, Baltimore, & Annapolis Electric Railroad terminal station. The railroad offered service for the South Shore Line as well as for Baltimore, Annapolis, and Washington D.C.

Cancelled 1917, $15-20

Longtime rivals of the Baltimore & Ohio Railroad, the Pennsylvania Railroad built Union Station in an attempt to outdo the Baltimore & Ohio's newly constructed Mount Royal Station.

Circa 1915, $6-8

Built section by section between 1857 and 1867, Camden Station was the first large passenger station built by Baltimore & Ohio Railroad. It was the location for the company's main offices for several years.

Cancelled 1916, $10-12

Union Station was buil: in 1911 and cost the Pennsylvania Railroad Company $750,000.

Circa 1910s, $8-9

Places to Stay

With so many different modes of travel coming together in one place, Baltimore saw a great number of visitors throughout the year. Various inns, hostelries, and boarding houses were built to accommodate visiting businessmen, sailors, and other travelers. By the time postcards were becoming popular, most of these small facilities had been torn down or destroyed in the Great Baltimore Fire. As the rest of the city modernized, Baltimore's hotels did the same. Larger more elegant hotels, like the Belvedere, the Southern, the Lord Baltimore, and the Emerson opened in the early twentieth century reflecting the glamour and sophistication of the time period and the people staying there.

The Baltimore and Ohio Railroad's *Royal Blue*—the "only diesel-powered train between Washington and New York."

Circa 1940s, $6-8

Situated on West Baltimore Street, the New Howard Hotel offered a number of comfortable rooms, a lunch special for fifty cents, and a full-course dinner for a dollar.

Circa 1915, $8-9

The Eutaw House, located on Eutaw and West Baltimore Streets. The Baltimore Orioles and visiting baseball teams would get dressed for games in this hotel.

Circa 1915, $7-8

In 1909, a waiter at the Belvedere Hotel informed millionaire Captain Isaac Emerson that he could not remove his jacket during dinner. Furious, Emerson stormed out of the hotel and swore that he would build his own hotel where he could do as wished. The Emerson Hotel was completed two years later in 1911.

Circa 1920s, $5-6

The Lobby of the Hotel Emerson. Reportedly, frogs from the ponds in the hotel's rooftop garden would hop off the roof and land on passersby below.

Circa 1915, $8-10

Known as "The Palace of the South," the Rennert Hotel was a meeting place for the city's Democratic politicians.

Circa 1915, $6-7

Opened in 1903, the Belvedere Hotel was known as the finest hotel in Baltimore and a number of notables including Mark Twain and Enrico Caruso were guests there.

Circa 1915, $6-7

The Southern Hotel was built on the site of the Fountain Inn and was opened during World War I.

Circa 1920s, $5-7

The Lord Baltimore Hotel on Hanover and Baltimore Streets. According to reports, the hotel is supposedly haunted.

Circa 1940s, $3-4

Also located on Hanover and Baltimore Streets, the Hotel Caswell was eventually demolished to make way for the Lord Baltimore Hotel.

Circa 1915, $6-7

Located on the fourteenth floor of the Southern Hotel, the "Spanish Villa" was home to live dance music, which was broadcast across the city as a nightly radio show.

Circa 1920s, $6-8

Places to See, Things to Do

Once visitors arrived in Baltimore, the question arose regarding what they were going to do while they were there. As with any urban center, there were a variety of attractions and diversions available to entertain and amuse tourists during their stay in Baltimore. Theatres like the Hippodrome and the Maryland Theatre offered plays and musicals. The Lyric Opera House showcased operas and other special events. Boasting impressive collections of ancient and modern art from around the world, The Baltimore Museum of Art and the Walters Art Gallery offered a rich vision of the art world. Sports fans could catch a football game at the Baltimore Stadium—the same stadium where the Baltimore Orioles won the International League World Series in 1944 and again in 1945. Every year, on the third Saturday in May, one of Baltimore's biggest sporting events, the Preakness Stakes, takes place. Held at the Pimlico Park Race Course, the Preakness Stakes is part of the Triple Crown of thoroughbred racing and always draws a large crowd to the city.

Home to the Baltimore Opera Company, the Lyric Opera House also hosts touring Broadway companies and other musical and cultural events.

Circa 1910s, $8-10

The Walters Art Gallery was built by Henry Walters and opened to the public in 1909. It was bequeathed to Baltimore in 1931 and houses the art collection that Walters had accumulated over forty years.

Circa 1940s, $3-4

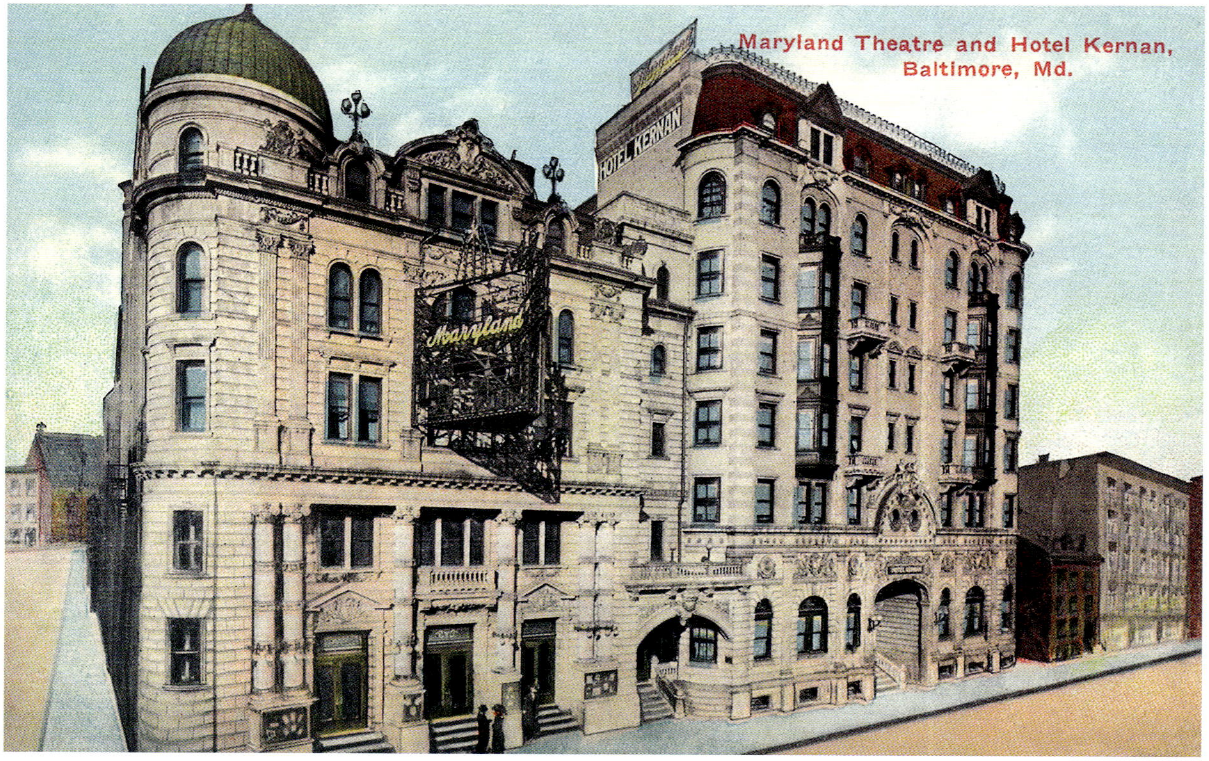

Actors and actresses performing in the Maryland Theatre would often stay at the Hotel Kernan next door.

Circa 1915, $8-10

An aerial view of the Baltimore Stadium. After Oriole Park burned down in 1944, the Baltimore Orioles played the rest of the season in Baltimore Stadium, winning the International League World Series there in 1944 and 1945.

Circa 1940s, $8-10

The Baltimore Hippodrome on Eutaw Street.

Circa 1915, $5-7

The gathering place of Baltimore's elite, the Maryland Country Club was located just outside the city.

Circa 1915, $7-8

The largest art museum in the state of Maryland, the Baltimore Museum of Art is home to collection of over 100,000 pieces of art.

Circa 1940s, $3-4

Opened in 1870, Pimlico Race Track is most famous for being the home of the Preakness, the second leg of the Triple Crown of Thoroughbred Horse Racing.

Circa 1920s, $8-9

A massive crowd of racing fans gather in the grandstands at Pimlico Race Track.

Circa 1920s, $8-9

Participants in the Maryland Hunt Cup Races jump fences on a racecourse near Baltimore. Held the last weekend in April, the race is the highlight of the steeplechase season in Maryland.

Circa 1940s, $5-6

Parks

In 1827, William Patterson, a prosperous Baltimore merchant, gave the city six acres of land on Hampstead Hill. These six acres would become Patterson Park, one of the oldest parks in Baltimore. This began somewhat of a trend, with the city purchasing or being given parcels of estates for the purpose of creating public parks. In 1860, the city purchased six hundred acres of land from Lloyd Rogers creating Druid Hill Park. Originally planned to be the location for the hospital and school he intended to fund, Johns Hopkins' summer estate, Clifton, was sold by the trustees of Hopkins' estate to the city and was turned into a public park.

Besides these, a number of other different kinds of parks were also established during that time period. One of the earliest amusement parks opened in Baltimore—the aptly named Electric Park—offered plays, rides, food and drink, boxing matches, and vaudeville acts, all under the brilliant glow of electric lights. Other amusement parks like Bay Shore Park, Carlin's Park, and the Gwynn Oak Park were also opened during that time period.

Skating on Druid Hill Park Lake was a popular activity for Baltimoreans during the winter months.

Circa 1915, $8-9

LAKE DRIVE, DRUID HILL PARK, BALTIMORE, MD.

Visitors get out and stretch their legs on Lake Drive in Druid Hill Park.

Circa 1940s, $3-5

CEDAR AVENUE BRIDGE OVER STONY RUN, NEAR DRUID HILL PARK, BALTIMORE, MD.

Cedar Avenue Bridge, located near Druid Hill Park.

Circa 1940s, $3-5

Built over Stony Run, the Cedar Avenue Bridge connects Wyman's and Druid Hill Parks.

Circa 1915, $3-4

Before it was a public park, Druid Hill Park was a private estate owned by the Rogers family. The mansion pictured here was built to replace the previous house, which burned down in 1796.

Circa 1915, $3-5

A view from the top of the Cedar Avenue Bridge.

Circa 1915, $3-5

From 1879 until 1945, the grounds around the Druid Hill Mansion were home to a flock of sheep. They can be seen here with "Mac," their shepherd.

Circa 1915, $7-8

Opened in 1876, the Baltimore Zoo is the second oldest zoo in the United States.

Circa 1940s, $3-4

Currently consisting of six hundred acres, Druid Hill Park was officially opened in October of 1860.

Circa 1915, $6-8

Silver Springs, one of the natural springs found in Druid Hill Park.

Circa 1915, $6-7

A Sunday crowd gathers to watch the antics of the sea lions in Druid Hill Park. The Sea Lion Pond was eventually drained and its inhabitants moved to new quarters inside the zoo.

Circa 1915, $6-8

The Centennial Fountain was erected in Druid Hill Park to celebrate the centennial anniversary of the founding of Baltimore.

Circa 1915, $5-7

Edmund's Well, where visitors could obtain fresh water from the spring beneath the monument.

Circa 1915, $6-7

Built in 1888, the Druid Hill Park Conservatory is believed to be one of the oldest conservatory buildings in the United States.

Circa 1940s, $3-4

Standing empty at the moment, the Druid Hill Park Bandstand eagerly awaits the next public concert.

Circa 1915, $5-6

Another view of the Druid Hill Lake Boathouse.

Circa 1930s, $3-5

In addition to ice skating on the frozen lake in the winter, Druid Hill Park Lake was very popular with visitors who liked to rent rowboats and canoes during warmer weather to relax out on the lake.

Circa 1930s, $3-5

Scene on the Lake,
Druid Hill Park, Baltimore Md.

LAKE ROLAND DAM, ROLAND PARK, BALTIMORE, MD.

Opposite page, top:
A moonlit scene on Druid Hill Park Lake.

Circa 1915, $5-7

A scene along Jones' Fall, a small park just outside the Baltimore's city limits.

Circa 1915, $5-6

The Mansion House at Carrole Park, one of several Baltimore estates that was sold or donated to the city to later became a public park.

Circa 1915, $6-8

Spectators gather to watch a swimming contest in Patterson Park.

Cancelled 1931, $7-8

Opposite page, bottom:
The Lake Roland Dam in Lake Roland Park.

Circa 1915, $5-6

The swimming pool at Patterson Park.

Circa 1915, $6-7

Called the "Pagoda" by the local population, the Patterson Park Observatory was designed and built by well-know architect, Charles Latrobe.

Circa 1915, $5-6

Like a number of other urban parks, Patterson Park was home to a casino, owned and operated by the city.

Circa 1915, $6-8

Before becoming a public park, Clifton Park was the summer home of Baltimore philanthropist, Johns Hopkins.

Circa 1915, $6-8

In 1895, the trustees of Hopkins' estate sold Clifton and the surrounding grounds to the city for $722,000.

Circa 1915, $6-8

Another scene in Riverside Park.

Circa 1920s, $3-5

Civil War cannons line a pathway in Riverside Park

Circa 1915, $6-8

Gwynn Oak Park was located outside of Baltimore at the end of the Powhattan Railroads Woodlawn Line.

Circa 1915, $8-10

Encompassing roughly 700 acres, Gwynn Falls Park is the largest park in Baltimore.

Circa 1920s, $3-5

Like its name implies, Bay Shore Park was located on the shore of the Chesapeake Bay and was only a short ferry ride away from Baltimore.

Circa 1915, $9-10

Made of concrete, the Bay Shore Park Pier extended a thousand feet into the Chesapeake Bay.

Circa 1915, $8-10

Besides ferry service, Bay Shore Park was also accessible by train.

Cancelled 1918, $6-7

A seafood dinner at the Colonial Dining Hall in the Bay Shore Park Casino cost about seventy-five cents per person.

Cancelled 1914, $6-8

Concertgoers gather at the Riverview Park Bandstand overlooking the Patapsco River.

Circa 1915, $6-9

A bird's eye view of the amusements at Carlin's Park.

Circa 1940s, $7-9

The Midway at Carlin's Park.

Circa 1920s, $10-12

Excursionists disembark from the steamer *Louise* at Tolchester Beach.

Circa 1915, $8-9

The entrance to Tolchester Beach. Tolchester Beach was a frequent destination for excursion steamers from Baltimore.

Circa 1915, $8-9

Woodland Hall, the administration offices for Forrest Park.

Circa 1915, $8-9

Opposite page, top: A view of some of the amusements that could be found at Electric Park.

Cancelled 1909, $9-10

Commanding an excellent view of the Harbor, Federal Hill was once the location of an observatory used for spotting ships that came into the Harbor. Federal Hill was made into a park in 1875.

Circa 1915, $6-7

Opposite page, bottom: Light bulbs put on a dazzling nighttime display at Electric Park, one of Baltimore's first amusement parks.

Circa 1915, $7-9

Electric Park, Baltimore, Md.

Electric Park
ELECTRIC PARK BY NIGHT, BALTIMORE, MD.
D-13 ILLUSTRATED POST CARD CO., N. Y.

Bibliography

Dorsey, John and James D. Dilts. *A Guide to Baltimore Architecture*. Centreville: Tidewater Publishers, 1997.

Males, Carolyn, Carol Barbier Rolnick, and Pam Makowskie Goresh. *Wish You Were Here: A Guide to Baltimore City for Natives and Newcomers*. Baltimore: Woodholme House Publishing, 1999.

Rowel, Melissa and Amy Lynwander. *Baltimore Harbor Haunts: True Ghost Stories*. Atglen: Schiffer Publishing, Ltd. 2005.

Shivers, Frank. "A Brief Baltimore History." Baltimore City Historical Society. http://www.historicbaltimore.org/shivers.htm. 1/18/06.

Smith, Bert. *Greetings From Baltimore: Postcard Views of the City*. Baltimore: The Johns Hopkins University Press, 1996.